MW01277224

2019 CANCER HOROSCOPE & ASTROLOGY

2019

Cancer

Horoscope & Astrology

Acknowledgment:

Thank you to the stargazers, dreamers, and

mystics.

You make this world a better place.

2019

Cancer

Horoscope & Astrology

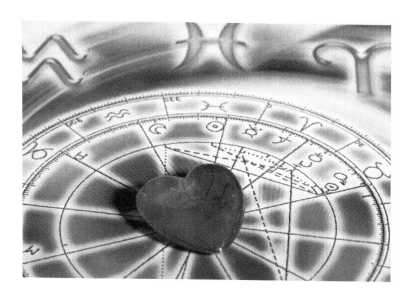

CANCER 2019 OVERVIEW

This is set to be a fortuitous year for Cancer. Three potent game-changing Supermoons move into Cancer's life in the first few months of 2019, this ensures plenty of potentials arrive to motivate Cancer to follow new leads. The first two Supermoons are in Leo, which puts a spotlight on relationships for Cancer, this indicates plenty of inspiration and innovative energy will be available to achieve stellar personal goals. The third Supermoon is also a rare Blue Moon, and this brings incredible mystical power into Cancer's emotional awareness.

There are miscommunications to navigate with Mercury Retrograde stirring the pot. Cancer can be oversensitive to these phases, so rebalancing your emotions are crucial.

2019 is a Power year, this dramatically alters Cancer's personal magic. When harnessed correctly, Cancer can make substantial progress towards the achievement of personal goals.

The final year of each decade holds the most considerable amount of power which can be utilized to manifest goals using the law of attraction. It has taken ten years to reach this level of personal control, and another Power year won't be coming along until 2029.

With so many compelling reasons to shine, Cancer can look forward to potent cosmic energy to boost the potential possible in 2019, and beyond.

JANUARY ASTROLOGY

January 1st – 5th - Quadrantids Meteor Shower.

The Quadrantids meteor shower run yearly from January 1st -5th. The Quadrantids meteor shower peaks on the night of the 3rd and morning of the 4th.

January 6th - New Moon in Capricorn.

This moon phase occurs at 01:28 UTC. This is an excellent time to star gaze as there is no moonlight.

January 6th - Venus with Greatest Western Elongation.

The planet Venus reaches it's highest eastern elongation of 47 degrees from the Sun.

January 6th - Partial Solar Eclipse.

This partial solar eclipse occurs in parts of eastern Asia and the northern Pacific Ocean.

January 14th – First Quarter Moon in Aries.

This Moon phase occurs at 06.45 UTC.

January 21st - Full Moon in Leo.

This full moon phase occurs at 05:16 UTC. This is known as the Full Wolf Moon because hungry wolf packs howled outside settlers camps. This full moon has also been identified as the Old Moon and the Moon After Yule.

January 21st - Supermoon.

This is the first of three super-moons for 2019.

January 21st - Total Lunar Eclipse.

This total lunar eclipse occurs in the majority of North America, South America, eastern Pacific Ocean, as well as the western Atlantic Ocean, extreme western Europe, and West Africa.

January 22nd - Conjunction of Venus and Jupiter.

A conjunction of Venus and Jupiter takes place with the two stunning planets within 2.4 degrees of each other in the pre-dawn sky.

January 27th – Last Quarter Moon in Scorpio.

This Moon phase occurs at 21.10 UTC.

JANUARY HOROSCOPE

JANUARY WEEK ONE

A new phase beckons and as you focus on the essentials you understand your most important goals on a deeper level. This provides you with added motivation and luck to begin a journey towards achieving significant growth. Opportunities pop up to support your dreams, and this leads to the turning of tides, you draw abundance into your surroundings. Realizing your own worth provides you with bold potential which touches every element of your life. True quality comes from within, recognizing your own value allows you to get clear about what you desire in your world. Following your own unique path enables you to express yourself creatively, you push your boundaries and explore broader horizons. Once your self-esteem is stable, you draw in support and resources from others who value your talents. This leads to a phase of deepening personal bonds and expressing your feelings to another with the open-heart. The January 6th New Moon in Capricorn contains welcome news.

11

JANUARY WEEK TWO

Listen carefully to your intuition and empathetic instincts. Your emotional awareness is guiding you towards a fresh start. After a phase of digging up old emotions and baggage, you release the heaviness and can embrace an exciting new path. Reflecting on the positive aspects launches you towards a new chapter of beautiful personal goals. An inspiring time is approaching which sees a celebration in the family. A few days later it brings you to a more reflective time. Thinking of past events provides you with a richness that is alluring. You are headed towards growth and can immerse yourself in exploring new endeavors which spark your interest. You benefit from the help of your closest allies, this shines a light on deepening bonds. Choosing wisely helps increase your sense of security on all levels. The First Quarter Moon in Aries brings valuable insight, this enables you to develop personal goals for the next phase of potential. This adds a sense of promise to your life.

JANUARY WEEK THREE

The Super Full Moon in Leo is guided to push out of your old comfort zone. Game-changing events sweep your inspiration up in new energy. This heralds the start of a fresh chapter of potential. Soon enough, you see positive signs that intimacy is occurring in your personal life. You may even hit the jackpot by developing a close bond with an individual who lights up your world, and this draws stability into your surroundings. This leads to an extended time which sees you emerge from doldrums and head towards a stellar chapter. Going back to basics sees you spend less time having to iron out hurdles which prevent progress. Making tweaks to your goals enables you to move forward more confidently towards the realization of your dreams. This puts a focus on the area of romantic potential and sees your situation shift towards a more happy phase. This week begins the start of heightened opportunity, it puts the spotlight on soul bonds and brings your life joy. The January 21st Total Lunar Eclipse holds a secret, as new information is illuminated.

JANUARY WEEK FOUR

Venus and Jupiter conjoin this week, change is in the air. You peel back the layers and get to the root of your dreams. Valuing yourself properly bolsters your self-esteem and leaves you in the correct frame of mind to develop an area of your life which holds significant meaning to you. You can put your focus on freedom and expansion as this revolutionizes your potential and delivers terrific outcomes into your world. Being swept away by the possibilities increases your enthusiasm for life. You are likely to break free of any constraints and dive into uncharted territory. This leads you towards an area of expansion and growth. Your intellectual mind and natural curiosity are sparked as you expand your horizons. You may even delve into a whole new philosophy and enter a phase of learning a new subject. Turning your intention on yourself heightens your ability to manifest what you need in your world. The January 27th Last Quarter Moon in Scorpio sees you take a vital step towards achieving a significant goal on your unique path.

FEBRUARY ASTROLOGY

February 4th - New Moon in Aquarius.

This Moon phase occurs at 21:03 UTC. This is an excellent time to star gaze as there is no moonlight to obscure your view of the universe.

February 12th – First Quarter Moon in Taurus.

This Moon phase occurs at 22.26 UTC.

February 19th - Full Moon in Leo.

This Moon phase occurs at 15:53 UTC. The February full moon is known as the Full Snow Moon because the heaviest snows usually fall during February. As hunting was difficult, this full moon has also been recognized as the Full Hunger Moon.

February 19th - Supermoon.

This is the second of three Supermoons for 2019. The Moon will be at its nearest approach to the Earth and will look slightly larger and brighter than usual.

February 26th – Last Quarter Moon in Sagittarius.

This Moon phase occurs at 11.28 UTC.

February 27th - Mercury at largest Eastern Elongation.

The planet Mercury reaches an eastern elongation of 18.1 degrees from the Sun.

FEBRUARY HOROSCOPE

FEBRUARY WEEK ONE

Focusing on your priorities enables you to embark on a task-driven week. An opportunity arrives which provides you with high-end potential. This sparks a new era of inspiration, and planting the seeds to develop this potential is a substantial boost to your situation. You can enjoy a bountiful week which shines a light on the area of teamwork and friendships. Collaborating with others creates rewarding bonds. You are able to make headway and gain a sense of clarity which allows you to release negativity. Honing in on your real purpose gives you happiness provides you with new and inspiring goals. A lucrative offer is revealed with the February 4th New Moon, and by examining your intentions, you can bolster your self-confidence and go for this opportunity. You can think about what your future goal is. Your plans stir the energy of manifestation and luminescent potential now arrives, which aligns with your dreams.

FEBRUARY WEEK TWO

There is news coming which is both exciting and daunting, it takes you towards a chapter which will require new levels of integrity, accountability, and personal development. It leads towards long-lasting security. A stable environment provides you with a solid foundation from which to further grow your talents. This opportunity will take time and effort, it leads towards tangible rewards. An expansive vision emerges through a time of contemplation. It is a phase of freedom-seeking, newfound energy arrives to entice you to explore broader horizons. A significant goal is nearing completion, it is the perfect time to reconnect with others and embrace social outings. An influential person plays a role in a memorable moment this week. Conversation occurs which feels soul-affirming and touches your heart on a deeper level. This leads to a chapter which marks a huge turning point for you, life is set to become sweeter. Someone special may pop into your life who holds potential for a meaningful connection. Nurturing the development of a significant situation brings your magic touch into play. Your practicality crowns this energy and creates robust potential.

FEBRUARY WEEK THREE

A chance encounter proves to be the catalyst for change, you solidify a connection which draws a significant promise into your world. It allows you to make clear decisions about your life as you take concrete action towards improving your circumstances. You make some functional changes and summon the strength to expand your horizons towards a chapter which glimmers with the potential. Revealing this chapter rebuilds your world. You are set to receive a positive sign that you are heading in the right direction. This signpost clearly indicates which area you should be concentrating on. This gives you a sense of purpose and aligns you correctly towards developing a significant situation which holds great promise. Building the right foundations provides you with objective feedback that you can tinker with, you understand this is how to grow your potential. This begins a wave of potential which involves wishes coming to fruition, or some kind of recognition for your talents.

FEBRUARY WEEK FOUR

Fresh energy is coming into the home and family-related matters. This is a great time to put into action ideas which support and nourish family members. Visualizing positive outcomes sets excellent intentions, and you will be able to see beneficial results unfold. Your positive energy helps usher in lovely potential, good things are likely to emerge for those you care about. Take time to share your creative ideas and thoughts with them. You connect with some influential people who resonate your frequency this week. The energy becomes downright electric, and this propels creativity towards a successful and innovative chapter. This gracefully supports your career and long-term goals. You break free of any limitations and incorporate new routines by planning helpful strategies. Sparking up fresh ideas leads to significant change and improvement in your circumstances. A lucky and expansive vista tempts you towards considerable variation and helps you take new steps towards a new personal journey. Unhook from anything which limits your self-expression.

MARCH ASTROLOGY

March 5th – Mercury Retrograde begins in Pisces.

During a retrograde period, it isn't the right time to move forward in any practical venture. Be prepared for misunderstandings and miscommunications to be prevalent. You can make plans during this time, but it may be best to put them into action after the retrograde ends.

March 6th - New Moon in Pisces.

This phase occurs at 16:04 UTC. This is an excellent time to observe galaxies and stars because there is no moonlight to interfere.

March 14th – First Quarter Moon in Gemini.

This Moon phase occurs at 10.27 UTC.

March 20th - March Equinox.

The March equinox takes place at 21:58 UTC. The Sun be shining on the equator, and there will be equal amounts of day and night throughout the world. This is the first day of spring (vernal equinox) in the Northern Hemisphere.

March 21ˢᵗ - Full Moon in Libra, Supermoon.

This full Moon is on the opposite side of the Earth as the Sun and shall be adequately illuminated. This phase occurs at 01:43 UTC. This full moon is known as the Full Worm Moon because this is the time of year when the ground softens, and earthworms reappear. This full moon is also known as the Full Crow Moon, the Full Crust Moon, the Full Sap Moon, and the Lenten Moon. This is also the last of three super-moons for 2019.

March 28ᵗʰ – Last Quarter Moon in Capricorn.

This Moon phase occurs at 22.26 UTC. April 15 –

March 28ᵗʰ - Mercury Retrograde ends in Pisces.

You can now move forward with any delayed plans that you have been putting off due to the Mercury Retrograde phase. Relationships should soon improve as tensions ease.

MARCH HOROSCOPE

MARCH WEEK ONE

You enter a phase of passion, creativity, and romance
soon. Obstacles are overcome in your personal life.
You find you click well with another. Consequently,
this leads to the development of a closer bond. In
addition to the wellspring of abundance and
harmony which flows into your world, you engage in
a highly introspective chapter. Relaxing and letting
things unfold in due time enables the layers of
potential to be revealed correctly. You are action
orientated and tend to take the lead, you are being
encouraged at this time to surrender and let the
universe guide your situation forward. You are
intuitively plugged into channels which provide you
with strong psychic flashes and intuitive abilities.
You are likely to usher in a chapter of expansion and,
positive outcomes soon. A meaningful journey sees
you head towards new found freedom. Being
reflective, not reactive is advised.

MARCH WEEK TWO

You are especially sensitive to cosmic vibrations this week, the planet Mercury went into retrograde late last week, and you begin to feel some cosmic fallout. You may be feeling especially sensitive at this time, and also richly creative, carving out for self-expression enables you to merge your spirit with your emotional stirrings. There may be a transition ahead which requires focused energy and concentration. This kicks off a first phase of achieving goals and planning for long-term dreams. An extensive time of broadening your horizons leaves you feeling giddy with potential. Personal matters play an important role soon, this puts the spotlight on authentic communication, and transparent dialogue. You evoke strong emotions in another, and the significance of this phase sees the development of a closer bond emerge.

Consequently, you begin to see signs that your circumstances are improving. In addition to this excellent outcome, you find yourself drawn towards having a meaningful conversation with someone who holds meaning to you. You are ready to embrace positive change.

MARCH WEEK THREE

There are astrological indications you will soon be the recipient of surprising news. The third full Supermoon of the year occurs in Libra this week, an opportunity arises soon which could call for a leap of faith or involve taking a bold risk. A turning point arrives, which enables you to deal with conflicting energy. With this in mind, you set an intention to resolve problematic power which has hindered progress recently. In light of new information which is revealed, you subsequently are able to transition towards a happier situation. Mending that which was broken isn't necessarily comfortable, or easy, but in the long run, it turns out to be a significant blessing. You are fiercely determined to improve your circumstances, you connect with someone whose strengths complement yours, this forms a formidable partnership. A period of reflection enables you to discern an opportunity which helps you overcome obstacles. Also, turning your thoughts to the past is primarily about dealing with unresolved issues. Retracing steps enables you to mend your spirit. Things come together in ways which are nothing short of brilliant.

MARCH WEEK FOUR

You enter a time of heightened efficiency and productivity, keeping busy enables your efforts to make a tangible difference to the goals you have in mind. As you pay attention to the plan in place, you meticulously organize your time effectively. Filtering out distractions and tuning in to a substantial goal enables your efforts to transition you to a new level of achievement. Important news arrives soon to provide you with insight into future potential. Someone with a complimentary skill set and synergistic energy is able to re-balance your emotions soon.

Furthermore, they assist you in developing a venture which is close to your heart. As a matter of fact, this is a bond which is unfurling in the most significant manner. Compelling evidence of a sense of sunshine emerging in your world is likely to give your spirit a boost. It is important to realize that you are being guided forward towards greener pastures.

APRIL ASTROLOGY

April 5th - New Moon in Aries.

This moon phase occurs at 08:51 UTC. This is an excellent time to observe galaxies and stars because there is no moonlight visible.

April 11th - Mercury at most substantial Western Elongation.

The planet Mercury reaches its most substantial western elongation of 27.7 degrees from the Sun.

April 12th – First Quarter Moon in Cancer.

This Moon phase occurs at 19.06 UTC.

April 19th - Full Moon in Libra.

The Moon is on the opposite side of the Earth as the Sun and will be completely illuminated. This moon phase occurs at 11:12 UTC. This full moon is known as Full Pink Moon because it marks the appearance of the first spring flowers. This full moon has also been identified as the Sprouting Grass Moon, the Growing Moon, and the Egg Moon. Many coastal areas call it Full Fish Moon because this was the time the fish swam upriver to breed.

April 22nd, 23rd - Lyrids Meteor Shower.

The Lyrids meteor shower runs each year from April 16-25. This meteor shower peaks on the night of the 22nd and the morning of the 23rd. These meteors sometimes produce bright dust trails that last for several seconds.

April 26th – Last Quarter Moon in Aquarius.

This Moon phase occurs at 22.18 UTC.

APRIL HOROSCOPE

APRIL WEEK ONE

It is an excellent week to set the positive intentions around realistic goals, as well as your most heartfelt desires. Committing to a plan creates a trajectory you can work along. Finding your work-life balance creates new security and stability. You shake off heavy emotional vibes and enjoy a lighter sense of harmony. Focusing on goals enables you to utilize unique creative abilities. You indulge in social activities which call to your spirit. A chance encounter begins the process of a situation which blossoms over the next six months. A few days after this meeting, you have some communication which is especially important. It brings up energy which leaves you feeling nostalgic. Tender sentiments are expressed which heighten your sensitive side. Give yourself extra time to process this emotional path as it does bring you to an enticing chapter of potential.

APRIL WEEK TWO

Implementing practical changes in your life enables a strong theme of stability and security to emerge. This brings a sense of satisfaction for the hard work and perseverance which provides you with growth. Potential skyrockets, this brings a revamping of dreams and goals. You focus on developing your unique talents, and this enables you to express an immensely creative side. New friends gravitate towards your circle bringing new potential into your world. Once you have a clear understanding of your path, you will be able to better focus your energies towards it. In time with a little progress, you will find a renewed sense of confidence that will allow you to take on challenges you once feared for in the past. This will bring out the best of you and will enable you to choose a road to happiness. You have a lot of good ahead so focusing on the good in your life and leaving the negative out will be significant. As you set your sights on future prospects, it inspires you to keep going.

APRIL WEEK THREE

The Full Moon in Libra this week is a time which sees you take stock of your progress thus far. Positive changes are coming, heightened motivation enable s you to put your goals front and center. As you develop a project which you hold dear, you take full advantage of a cycle of improved energy. It is time to enjoy soul driven inspiration which has the power to rejuvenate your life and reawaken your spirit. Nurturing your goals provides you with valuable emotional sustenance. Relevant information is set to arrive soon. You may feel guided to look back at the past, this is a time of processing heavy emotions, dealing with closure, and revisiting previous situations. This week brings you to a turning point, an essential phase of cleansing and rejuvenation. Conducting a personal inventorying enables your life to transition to a brighter phase. Once the own baggage is dealt with, you reboot your potential. Your motivation runs high, a new opportunity sparks interest.

APRIL WEEK FOUR

A message arrives which speaks of significant opportunities arrives linked to the areas of growth, business, and good fortune. You embark on a thrilling chapter which provides you with a fresh start that is deeply personal to you. Setting intentions to surrender to the potential possible enables you to dissolve old feelings of mistrust and doubt. This paves the way for long-term growth and success to occur. You enter a phase of news and communications this week, which bring word about a long-awaited development. The potential is exceptional as it is the combination of something you have been working towards and a long-held aspiration. This culminates in a ground-breaking conversation with a kindred spirit. You wrap up loose ends and embrace beginning a new chapter of potential. Consequently, your outlook is on the rise, positive outcomes are indicated.

MAY ASTROLOGY

May 4th - New Moon in Taurus.

This phase occurs at 22:46 UTC. The new moon phase is a brilliant time to observe galaxies and stars because there is no moonlight visible.

May 6th, 7th - Eta Aquarids Meteor Shower.

The Eta Aquarids meteor shower runs annually from April 19 to May 28. It peaks this year on the night of May 6 and the morning of the May 7.

May 12th – First Quarter Moon in Leo.

This Moon phase occurs at 01.12 UTC.

May 18th - Full Moon in Scorpio, Blue Moon.

The Moon is on the opposite side of the Earth as the Sun, and its face will be fully illuminated. This phase occurs at 21:11 UTC. The May full moon is known as the Full Flower Moon because this is when spring flowers are in abundance. This full moon is also known as the Full Corn Planting Moon and the Milk Moon. This year it is also a blue moon. This unusual calendar event only happens once every few years, giving rise to the term, "once in a blue moon." There are usually three full moons in each season. A fourth full moon is called a Blue moon and occurs on average once every 2.7 years.

May 26ᵗʰ – Last Quarter Moon in Aquarius.

This Moon phase occurs at 16.33 UTC.

MAY HOROSCOPE

MAY WEEK ONE

Life has thrown you a curve-ball at times, but you are adaptive and capable. While you have known dramatic upheaval, this has become the strength from which you now propel yourself forward. Following your dreams enables you to be your truth, the universe has got your back. You take a vital step towards achieving a significant goal in your unique journey soon. You may have been through a psychologically fraught time recently, but you are set to see the brighter side of life again. Focusing on developing your future can see miracles happen. You channel your optimism towards a new area which holds promise. This draws terrific potential into your world. You can look forward to an enticing chapter which captivates your imagination and sets the ball rolling for future progress.

MAY WEEK TWO

You are evolving into your real potential. Your life is taking you full speed ahead, and you can kick off to a fresh area of growth soon. New opportunities allow you to make great strides which remove current limits. Reflect and acknowledging how far you have come. You can make the most of this time, and people are willing to support your dreams. You are a warrior who makes your world so much bigger and bolder. You have strong powers of focus and productivity this week which enable you to head towards significant growth. Releasing fear lets you expand your horizons in great directions. You have a desire to learn and thrive on being inspired by new ideas and projects. Finding a venture for those lofty visions will be beneficial to your overall progress.

MAY WEEK THREE

A rare Blue Full Moon occurs in Scorpio this week. This is a time which focuses on family, and foundations. You embrace sharing time with the closest members of your tribe, a night of bonding nurtures your soul. An opportunity arises, which allows you to learn a new skill. This leads to a time of expanding your horizons and embracing positive changes which seek to inspire your awareness. Opening the door to new experiences heightens well-being and brings joy into your world. Opportunities for growth and learning emerge, this may take the shape of a new hobby which is inspiring and captivates your imagination. It provides you with a sense of achievement. You begin to perceive a broader picture of what may be possible, indicating there is a more immense potential available. This is a time which sees your life change in positive ways, a flow of energy arrives to motivate you towards developing substantial goals.

MAY WEEK FOUR

You are entering a time of heightened potential in the area of communication. As the sun illuminates this opportunity, you are likely to be drawn to moving out of your comfort zone and beginning a new chapter of potential with your love interest. Opening your heart fully to sharing positive energy with this person has a magnetizing effect. This draws you both together in a natural way and allows the situation to unfold over time. This character may have been holding back feelings, they are likely to express themselves authentically to you soon. An extra, heartfelt and emotional discussion channels their intensity across to you. This clears away any old issues and brings harmony back to the situation. It paves the way for the development of a better connection. You will feel that the energy has become much more transparent and lighter with this person.

Singles enter a week of heightened ability to draw new love into their life. Stay open to meaningful coincidences which guides a connection into being.

June 3rd - New Moon in Gemini.

This moon phase occurs at 10:02 UTC. This is an excellent time to observe galaxies and stars because there is no moonlight to interfere.

June 10t – First Quarter Moon in Virgo.

This Moon phase occurs at 05.59 UTC.

June 10th - Jupiter at Opposition.

The planet Jupiter will be at its nearest approach to Earth, and its planet face will be illuminated entirely by the Sun.

June 17th - Full Moon in Sagittarius.

The Full Moon is on the opposite side of the Earth as the Sun, and its face will be completely illuminated. This moon phase occurs at 08:31 UTC. This full moon is known as Full Strawberry Moon because it is the peak of strawberry harvesting season. The June Full Moon has also been identified as the Full Rose Moon and the Full Honey Moon.

e 21st - June Solstice.

The June solstice occurs at 15:54 UTC. The North Pole will be tilted toward the Sun, which, having reached its northernmost position in the sky will be over the Tropic of Cancer at 23.44 degrees north latitude. This heralds the first day of summer (summer solstice) in the Northern Hemisphere, and is considered one of the most influential times of the year for many traditional cultures.

June 23rd - Mercury at largest Eastern Elongation.

The planet Mercury reaches most substantial eastern elongation of 25.2 degrees from the Sun.

June 25th – Last Quarter Moon in Aries.

This Moon phase occurs at 09.46 UTC.

JUNE HOROSCOPE

JUNE WEEK ONE

News arrives to inspire your imagination, to motivate you out of your usual routine. You enter an enticingly expansive time where dreams are possible. This bountiful chapter contains an unusually high number of personal interactions and puts your focus towards making long-term plans. It is a considerable time for networking and talking about the future as well as making things happen in your world. You bring creativity and innovation to this process. Fantastic opportunities to spread your wings ignite your spirit. You reveal exciting opportunities which keep your mind open to new potential. Sharing your creative ideas with a broader audience indicates you can capitalize on this fortuitous environment. You get busy crafting your dreams into something tangible. This provides you with new treasures of inspiration and motivates you to keep aspiring to improve your world.

JUNE WEEK TWO

The planet Jupiter reaches its closest approach to the earth this week. It will be at its brightest, and this illuminates a sign which leads you to an altruistic path. Your personal energy increases soon, and this allows you to develop goals with a lovely rhythm. You live entirely and connect to life. Gratitude is a driving force, and it does attract abundance into your life. Your whole perspective is drawing earthly delights into your world. The more you appreciate what is available, the more you see your horizons expanding. A nice windfall is likely soon. Working with your powers of visualization and manifestation to attract the right situation into your life. One of your creative ideas does draw great potential and takes you far. Your likely to head towards a busy time this week which motivates you to build new growth and bring stability into your life. Focusing on priorities now allows you to hone in on your most important life goals. This is a lucrative phase which attracts abundance.

JUNE WEEK THREE

There will be an opportunity to travel down memory lane with a cherished friend soon. You move to a chapter which involves social connections and group activities. This sees your spirits becoming exceptionally high, and you can indulge in heightened opportunities to connect with others. You find value in being generous and open with your time. This fires are community-minded collaborations and see you make headway towards a happier environment. You have been going through a difficult time, you will overcome these hurdles and achieve a more comfortable situation in your life. It may be difficult for you to see the bigger picture at this time but you are being guided to develop your personal life. Information is coming soon which will enable you to see a clear direction to head towards.

JUNE WEEK FOUR

You can expect heightened opportunities for creativity and self-expression. Finding yourself in a group gives you the opportunity to develop meaningful bonds. Building in more time for yourself helps you build the right foundations for future growth. This could see you reconnect with someone cherished or see you try learning new skills. You enjoy valuable time with your nearest and dearest. The foundations you build will provide you with ample opportunity to weave blessings into your world. This sees bigger doors open for you and you draw a profound bond with another into your world. Spending time with friends enable plans to emerge which puts your focus on exciting endeavors. Opportunities to collaborate provide you with a valuable sense of kinship.

January 1st – 5th - Quadrantids Meteor Shower.

July 2nd - New Moon in Cancer.

This moon phase occurs at 19:16 UTC. This is an excellent time to observe galaxies and stars because there is no moonlight visible.

July 2nd - Total Solar Eclipse.

The total solar eclipse occurs in parts of the southern Pacific Ocean, central Chile, and central Argentina. A partial eclipse is visible in the Pacific Ocean and western South America.

July 7th – Mercury Retrograde begins in Leo.

During a retrograde period, it isn't the right time to move forward in any practical venture. Be prepared for misunderstandings and miscommunications to be prevalent.

July 9th – First Quarter Moon in Libra.

This Moon phase occurs at 10.55 UTC.

July 9th - Saturn at Opposition.

The beautiful ringed planet Saturn will be at its nearest approach to Earth, and it will be illuminated by the Sun.

July 16th - Full Moon in Capricorn.

The July Full Moon is located on the opposite side of the Earth as the Sun and will be fully illuminated. This phase occurs at 21:38 UTC. This full moon is known as Full Buck Moon because the male buck deer start to grow new antlers. This full moon is also known as the Full Thunder Moon and the Full Hay Moon.

July 16th - Partial Lunar Eclipse.

The partial lunar eclipse will be visible throughout most of Europe, Africa, central Asia, and the Indian Ocean.

July 25th – Last Quarter Moon in Taurus.

This Moon phase occurs at 01.18 UTC.

July 28th, 29th - Delta Aquarids Meteor Shower.

The Delta Aquarids meteor shower peaks on the night of July 28 and morning of July 29.

July 31ˢᵗ - Mercury Retrograde ends in Cancer.

You can now move forward with any delayed plans that you have been putting off due to the Mercury Retrograde phase. Relationships should soon improve as tensions ease.

JULY HOROSCOPE

JULY WEEK ONE

You may have gone through a difficult time, but you can improve your circumstances with a clear plan and persistence. You are someone who radiates inner strength and capabilities. Your drive to succeed is unstoppable, and your talents are likely to receive recognition soon. Choose your goals carefully, place your aim, and go for it. It is an excellent time to move forward and make strategic connections which provide you with fresh leads. Networking enables you to plot your ascent towards the achievement of a significant goal. Harness the inspiration you felt earlier in the year and put your grand ideas into action. You have made excellent progress so far, and the best is yet to come.

JULY WEEK TWO

You have some uncertainty and doubt. It is natural when moving out of your comfort zone to feel a sense of disquiet. You are on a path to obtaining personal growth and development of spirit. Only you can intrinsically know if this is meant to be. You will be given a strong sign once you meet this person. Your intuition is more than willing to guide you on this journey. Trust in the process and let go of fixed expectations. A reprieve from intensity is coming up for you soon. This puts the spotlight on new potential in your personal life. It takes you to a turning point and enables you to renew your spirit and focus on developing your world in a meaningful manner. This is the perfect time to indulge in self-care and relaxation. There is no need to rush ahead, the journey is the destination which draws inspiration into your world.

JULY WEEK THREE

It is in the disquiet and the unsettling vibrations that you find your correct path. You are headed towards a time of transition which sees your potential jump to a new level. You are being urged to expand your perception of what you have thought was possible. This could take you towards learning a new area and in doing so brings you in contact with the one who makes your heart sing. You are on the path towards self-improvement. Baggage from the past can weigh heavily on your shoulders. Remember, you've got to release old situations which limit your progress. You might experience a rush of neediness soon which blurs the edges of your personal goals. Taking time to reflect, provides you with valuable insight which will enable you to set your intentions correctly. Once you have your goals, start taking concrete actions to make your vision a reality.

JULY WEEK FOUR

You work to make the best of your situation. You are gifted with perseverance and determination. You may have experienced setbacks, but you are able to reveal new areas to provide you with growth. Double check everything, you are set to enter a time which is driven by growth and abundance. This sees you get the wind back in your sails. You are on the path towards a higher calling. Living a life of purpose provides you with a sense of achievement and abundance. Your compassionate heart is able to make a difference in the lives of others who need your gifts. The difficulties of the past become part of your spirit and provide you with a type of empathy which is extraordinary. You are dedicated to not only improve your life but also, others in need. The Delta Aquarids Meteor shower this week provides you with energy which is revitalizing and tantalizing. Your personal magic helps transform your prospects for the better.

AUGUST ASTROLOGY

August 1st - New Moon in Leo.

This moon phase occurs at 03:12 UTC. This is an excellent time to observe galaxies and stars because there is no moonlight to interfere.

August 7th – First Quarter Moon in Scorpio.

This Moon phase occurs at 17.31 UTC.

August 9th - Mercury at most substantial Western Elongation.

The planet Mercury reaches greatest western elongation of 19.0 degrees from the Sun.

August 12th, 13th - Perseids Meteor Shower.

The Perseids meteor shower runs each year from July 17 to August 24. It peaks this year on the night of August 12 and the morning of August 13.

August 15th - Full Moon in Aquarius.

The August Full Moon is located on the opposite side of the Earth as the Sun and will be fully illuminated. This phase occurs at 12:30 UTC. The August full moon is known as the Full Sturgeon Moon because sturgeon fish of the Great Lakes and other major lakes are plentiful. This full moon has also been identified as the Green Corn Moon and the Grain Moon.

August 23rd – Last Quarter Moon in Taurus.

This Moon phase occurs at 14.56 UTC.

August 30 - New Moon in Virgo.

This moon phase occurs at 10:37 UTC. This is an excellent time to view galaxies and stars because there is no moonlight to interfere.

AUGUST HOROSCOPE

AUGUST WEEK ONE

This week you find yourself busy and achieve a great deal of progress on a venture you are working on. Something special comes into your life to broaden your horizons thrillingly. You may decide to launch a visionary endeavor this week as your confidence, and positive thinking is at an all-time high. Heading out on your own hero's journey provides you with the soul-affirming feedback you are destined for great things. You are transitioning to a new chapter which will give you a beneficial environment. Change is difficult and can feel unsettling, but the results are worthwhile. You'll find yourself inspired by fresh ideas and new possibilities, it turns your creative thoughts into gold. This shines a light on your expansive and optimistic side. You find that a grand idea does come to fruition and something which broadens your horizons brings joy.

AUGUST WEEK TWO

This is an intense week for personal growth, you can plant the seeds of a new vision which blossoms over the next few months. Changes definitely in the air, this enables you to strengthen your ideas, and begin to make progress, as you cross the bridge towards a more fulfilling chapter. Re-vamping your social life allows you to touch base with an inspiring individual who captures your imagination and entices you out of your comfort zone. This can be a life-changing chapter for you so far as your hopes and dreams for the future are concerned. You should find that delays will end, and all communication improves, so you can reach out and brainstorm with another. A joint project will either be born in your personal life, or good progress will be made in something you plan.

AUGUST WEEK THREE

Hurdles of the past do not diminish you, they make you stronger and able to identify areas of your life which hold promise. Protecting your precious energy provides you with fantastic potential for growth. Releasing negativity focuses on abundance and does draw new potential into your world. Keep an eye out for information which is specifically meant for you. You will intuitively know this is the right direction through a sense of synchronicity. You benefit from revisiting an old project this week. Community opportunities can offer promise and lead to lively discussions. Taking your filters down provides you with glimpses of significant potential. You are seeking greener pastures and now can draw harmonious energy into your world. Life is set to be brighter and does offer you exciting chances to move in a new direction. A happy surprise is expected soon.

AUGUST WEEK FOUR

Focusing on key people and projects provide you with a head start on a beneficial area which is set to blossom. A social invitation grabs your attention and gets you involved in an adventurous time out. Connecting with someone who is fully attentive and offers you sublime energy makes this situation profoundly intimate. You enjoy the journey and can embrace developing a stronger connection with this charismatic individual. Enticing information reaches you which places your focus on the area of intimacy and long-term security. You become concerned with more profound emotions and higher aspects of life. An individual arrives to entice you to live life to the fullest. This has the potential to become a soul bond, and your perceptions are especially keen on this character. You navigate emotional complexity with grace and composure. It shines a spotlight on your dreams for the future.

SEPTEMBER ASTROLOGY

September 9th - Neptune at Opposition.

The giant blue planet will be at its closest approach to Earth, and its face will be illuminated by the Sun.

September 6th – First Quarter Moon in Sagittarius.

This Moon phase occurs at 03.10 UTC.

September 14th - Full Moon in Pisces.

The September full Moon is on the opposite side of the Earth as the Sun, and its face will be fully illuminated. This phase occurs at 04:34 UTC. This full moon is known as the Full Corn Moon because the corn is harvested around this time. This full moon is also called the Harvest Moon which is the full moon that occurs nearest to the September equinox each year.

September 22nd – Last Quarter Moon in Gemini.

This Moon phase occurs at 02.41 UTC.

September 23rd - September Equinox.

The 2019 September equinox occurs at 07:50 UTC. The Sun shines directly on the equator, creating equal amounts of day and night throughout the world. This is also the first day of fall (autumnal equinox) in the northern hemisphere and is considered a significant zodiac event for many cultures.

September 28th **- New Moon in Virgo.**

This phase occurs at 18:26 UTC. This is an excellent time to observe galaxies and stars because there is no moonlight visible.

SEPTEMBER HOROSCOPE

SEPTEMBER WEEK ONE

Doors are set to open, networking with others stirs up a dialogue which influences your ability to attract the interest of a meaningful partner. This sees you being able to move forward towards developing a closer bond. It is a great time to stretch the barriers of your comfort zone by meeting new people and exploring social activities. The energy around your life becomes lighter and much more social, leading to expansive opportunities in your personal life. You can move forward towards developing your dreams. Remember to allow yourself to become emotionally vulnerable when a situation is unfolding, as this will enable you to take a step forwards towards bonding. Opening your heart ensures bonds blossom, you have beautiful gifts of self-expression and sharing your thoughts with another leads you to the highest outcome. Expect news to arrive soon which provides you with insight.

SEPTEMBER WEEK TWO

The planet Neptune is at its closest approach to Earth this week, it will be at its brightest, this really gets the creative juices flowing for you. The difficulties you have faced in the past have awakened your inner warrior. Your presence has become stronger, revitalizing your spirit, you are ready to break through to new potential and make the most of the opportunities which arrive to tempt you out of your comfort zone. One person, in particular, holds the key to your emotional awareness. This suggests a powerful transformation occurs which becomes the turning point for the next phase of your life. As you branch out and meet new people, you enter a busy and industrious chapter. Meeting someone who inspires you raises the prospect of developing closer bonds. It puts you in a light-hearted frame of mind and creates a nice break away from your usual routine. This invigorates your social life and sparks a refreshing chapter of developing emotional awareness. It is a great time to banish doubt and embrace change.

SEPTEMBER WEEK THREE

This week illuminates a desire which you find most tempting. It suggests you use a contemplative time to reflect on your goals and plans. Are corrections in order or are you able to manifest that which you dream about? It does point to an area of transformation, intimacy, and merging of souls. It is especially potent as it can lead to significant change. Intense emotions guide your awareness forward. You are entering a time of increasing potential, if you channel that intensity into your highest path, you achieve a productive result. This is a beautiful time for taking action towards the realization of long-term goals, you can prepare for the planting and tending of your seeds of manifestation. This is an extensive week which holds the promise of robust growth. Confidence issues can be released, prepare to shine.

SEPTEMBER WEEK FOUR

The Equinox this week indicates growth opportunities arriving soon. You may have created a new life for yourself from the ground up and are consequently required to plan new goals. You will quickly reap the rewards of new opportunities by prioritizing your main focus on an area which is in alignment with your heart's calling. In addition to the discussion, you obtain real benefits through self-expression and creative undertakings. Valuable lessons from the past guide this crucial phase of personal growth. There are some subtle yet beautiful changes for you within the next month. You will discover new people with excellent and exciting opportunities coming your way, but you need to be patient and allow it to happen at its own pace. Once you are able to throw caution to the wind, you will see changes coming back to you in the form of many rewards on different levels

October 8th - Draconids Meteor Shower.

The Draconids meteor shower runs annually from October 6-10 and peaks this year on the night of the 8th.

October 5th – First Quarter Moon in Capricorn.

This Moon phase occurs at 16.47 UTC.

October 13th - Full Moon in Aries.

The October full Moon is on the opposite side of the Earth as the Sun, and its face will be fully illuminated. This phase occurs at 21:09 UTC. This full moon is known as the Hunters Moon because at this time of year the leaves are falling, and game animals are plentiful. This full moon is also known as the Travel Moon and the Blood Moon.

October 20th - Mercury at Greatest Eastern Elongation.

The planet Mercury reaches greatest eastern elongation of 24.6 degrees from the Sun.

October 21st – Last Quarter Moon in Cancer.

This Moon phase occurs at 12.39 UTC.

October 21st, 22nd - Orionids Meteor Shower.

The Orionids meteor shower runs yearly from October 2 to November 7. Orionids meteor shower peaks this year on the night of October 21 and the morning of October 22.

October 27th - Uranus at Opposition.

The planet Uranus will be at its nearest approach to Earth, and its face will be illuminated by the Sun.

October 28th - New Moon in Scorpio.

This moon phase occurs at 03:39 UTC. This is an excellent time of the month to view galaxies and stars because there is no moonlight visible.

October 31st – Mercury Retrograde begins in Scorpio.

During a retrograde period, it isn't the right time to move forward in any practical venture. Be prepared for misunderstandings and miscommunications to be prevalent.

OCTOBER HOROSCOPE

OCTOBER WEEK ONE

Your awareness of subtle energy is heightened, intuition is available to help you with situations, especially with business dealings. You may receive word about a lucrative deal, or income opportunity this week. Your businesses reach a turning point, enabling the development of a new level of growth. Your communication skills lead to further networking and opportunities for robust endeavors. You set out to engage in a productive and ambitious chapter. It is work related, you make essential headway in developing your goals. You enter a time which places a robust emphasis on productivity and potential. Sharing ideas and meeting with others sees you network beneficially. It is an excellent time for pitching purposes and growth.

OCTOBER WEEK TWO

This week draws sheer brilliance into your world. Your curious nature thrives in the intellectually current climate ahead. This provides you with plenty of lively energy. You catch up with friends for a social outing, it's an excellent time to share thoughts and ideas with others. Getting involved in the community provides you with plenty of opportunities to draw well-being into your world. Sharing your insights and wisdom helps another person close to you. You spend time with people who stimulate your mind, this enables the conversation to flow freely as they are on your wavelength. The discussions which emerge plant the seeds for some exciting new plans. This kicks off a substantial cycle of potential. It heralds expansion and transformation, as highly creative energy is making itself known to you. A new venture soothes your restless soul. You yearn for a deepening bond, this is coming soon.

OCTOBER WEEK THREE

You enter a time where there can be misunderstandings or a communication fail. This could lead to a lack of harmony. Watching out for problematic situations allows you to think twice before putting the message out, a tactical approach provides for a swift resolution. An inspirational project arrives to clear the air and enable you to brainstorm with friends. There is cosmic energy surrounding this opportunity. A missing piece of a puzzle is revealed soon, as more profound emotions around intimacy, vulnerability and commitment are resolved. As you acknowledge the layers of awareness which cloak your spirit, you transform your potential. Diving into the depths of your inner realm removes blocks and fears. There is a whole new chapter waiting to unfurl itself, this is a time of transformation and evolution. An opportunity arrives, which leads to self-expression.

OCTOBER WEEK FOUR

The planet Uranus will be at its closest approach to Earth this week. An opportunity to flex your wings leads to an extensive time. You gain the attention of another who seeks to develop a closer bond. You enjoy being around people and it is a week of one-on-one interactions. It is a time which boosts your dreams to a new level and brings raw potential into your world. You become more confident and enjoy the harmonious interactions which bring sweetness into your world. An idea comes to fruition, and this is something that does excitingly broaden your horizons. Your confidence and positive thinking improve as you hear the whispers of your heart urging you to expand your world. This leads to an epiphany about something that makes sense, you gain clarity, and in a much-needed moment of honesty, you can embrace the authentic dialogue which is coming from within your spirit. You begin to see the world differently.

NOVEMBER ASTROLOGY

November 4th – First Quarter Moon in Aquarius.

This Moon phase occurs at 10.23 UTC.

November 5th, 6th - Taurids Meteor Shower.

The Taurids meteor shower runs yearly from September 7 to December 10. It peaks this year on the night of November 5.

November 11th - Rare Transit of the planet Mercury Across the Sun.

The planet Mercury moves directly between the Earth and the Sun. This is a rare event that occurs only once every few years. The next transit of Mercury does not take place until 2039.

November 12th - Full Moon in Taurus.

The November full Moon is on the opposite side of the Earth as the Sun, and its face will be fully illuminated. This phase occurs at 13:36 UTC. This full moon is known as Full Beaver Moon as this was the time of year beaver traps were used. It is also known as the Frosty Moon and the Hunter's Moon.

November 17th, 18th - Leonids Meteor Shower.

The Leonids meteor shower runs yearly from November 6-30. The Leonids meteor shower peaks this year on the night of the 17th and morning of the 18th.

November 19th – Last Quarter Moon in Leo.

This Moon phase occurs at 21.11 UTC.

November 20th - Mercury Retrograde ends in Scorpio.

You can now move forward with any delayed plans that you have been putting off due to the Mercury Retrograde phase. Relationships should soon improve as tensions ease.

November 24th - Conjunction of Venus and Jupiter.

A conjunction of Venus and Jupiter is visible on November 24. The two planets are within 1.4 degrees of each other in the night sky.

November 26th - New Moon in Scorpio.

This phase occurs at 15:06 UTC. This is an excellent time to view galaxies and star clusters because there is no moonlight visible.

November 28th - Mercury at Greatest Western Elongation.

The planet Mercury obtains western peak elongation of 20.1 degrees from the Sun.

NOVEMBER HOROSCOPE

NOVEMBER WEEK ONE

This is a significant time for you emotionally as healthy change is possible. You are being supported to fulfill your dreams and develop your life in a manner which is in alignment with your hearts calling. A relationship may be evolving, this sees the sparks of potential flying. A celebration or group activity helps bring a bond to the forefront of your mind. Exciting visions of what may be possible allow you to dream big. There is a need this week to take care of unfinished business. It is a time which is thoughtful and sees improvement in the areas of communication and social life. This breathes new life into your world. Connecting with new people may even draw a kindred spirit who entices you to deepen the connection. Inspiration strikes and shines a light on raw potential. This leaves you feeling expansive about the future.

NOVEMBER WEEK TWO

This week the planet Mercury makes a rare transit across the Sun. As it moves between the Sun and the Earth, it fires up your consciousness, you sweep away that which no longer serves you. You are transitioning to a chapter which puts the spotlight on long-term personal goals. This takes you to an extensive and lucky time. Broadening your perception of what is possible enables you to gracefully move towards developing a bond which is profound, emotional, and rewarding. As this situation holds true potential, it also supports your well-being. Focusing on your priorities spells out a clear intention of what you hope to achieve. You are set to benefit from changes in your social group, activities arrive which sees you honestly in your element. This is a chapter which is made for networking, you enjoy lively discussions with kindred spirits. Being around like-minded souls livens up your life, and you forge a deeper active connection with someone meaningful to you. Keep open to new areas which arrive soon to inspire you

NOVEMBER WEEK THREE

New beginnings are coming, and an influential person could figure into future events and perhaps open a door for you to a new chapter of potential. Life is becoming smoother, and though you have down with many hurdles, this only has increased resilience and strength of character. Finding ways to express your spirit provides you with a beneficial outlet. You are highly creative and have talents which allow your real personality to shine. You have gifts of supporting and nurturing others. I do see things coming together for you soon. This segues into a chapter which is more adventurous and emphasizes your desire to be the change you want to see in the world. This is a journey which begins a fresh episode of potential, it is an emotional voyage at times and does build up into an endeavor you can be proud of. You can embrace embarking on this path of action.

NOVEMBER WEEK FOUR

Synchronicity abounds in your life, staying alert for these signs from the divine enable you to obtain essential guidance. You enter a chapter which focuses on self and identity, and you are highly creative. You transition to a phase of new beginnings. Making solid plans towards personal goals and endeavors gives you robust rewards. The opportunity to engage in a meaningful venture puts your focus on developing a partnership. You enter a phase of rest and closure which puts you in a quieter, more introspective mood. Dialing down commitments enables you to use this time to take stock of your life. Re-balancing your energy is soothing and healing, it soon heralds the beginning of a fresh slate of potential. This is a time of transition where you commit to letting go of the past and shed old skins. Releasing leads to rejuvenation of spirit. Positive news arrives this week to bless you.

DECEMBER ASTROLOGY

December 4th – First Quarter Moon in Pisces.

This Moon phase occurs at 06.58 UTC.

December 12th - Full Moon in Gemini.

The Moon is on the opposite side of the Earth as the Sun, and its face will be fully illuminated. This moon phase occurs at 05:14 UTC. This full moon is known as the Full Cold Moon because this is when chilly winters air arrives and nights become long and dark. This full moon is also known as the Long Nights Moon and the Moon Before Yule.

December 13th, 14th - Geminids Meteor Shower.

The Geminids meteor shower runs each year from December 7-17. The Geminids meteor showers peaks this year on the night of the 13th and morning of the 14th.

December 19th – Last Quarter Moon in Virgo.

This Moon phase occurs at 04.57 UTC.

December 22nd - December Solstice.

The 2019 December solstice occurs at 04:19 UTC. The South Pole of the earth tilts toward the Sun, which, having reached its most southern place in the sky, is directly over the Tropic of Capricorn at 23.44 degrees south latitude. This December solstice also marks the first day of winter (winter solstice) in the Northern Hemisphere.

December 21st, 22nd - Ursids Meteor Shower.

The Ursids meteor shower occurs each year from December 17 - 25. This meteor event peaks this year on the night of the 21st and morning of the 22nd.

December 26th - New Moon in Capricorn.

This moon phase occurs at 05:15 UTC. This is an excellent time to view galaxies and stars because there is no moonlight visible.

December 26th - Annular Solar Eclipse.

An annular solar eclipse occurs because the Moon is too far away from the Earth to adequately hide the Sun. This results in a ring of light around the dark Moon. The Sun's corona is not visible during an annular eclipse.

DECEMBER HOROSCOPE

DECEMBER WEEK ONE

An invitation arrives which puts your focus on your most personal goals and desires. Planning passion projects enable you to heighten the potential. Setting intentions for growth inspires you to revamp and rejuvenate your social life. You enter a phase which is highly productive, practical, and capable. The strong potential is emerging in your social life, and this could result in a blissful moment of bonding with another. There are new chances to collaborate with another soon, this is a cooperative venture which allows your dreams to soar. Working in sync with someone who holds meaning to you is a beautiful way of sharing and developing a closer bond. As you pool together talents, you create incredible potential. Problem-solving overcomes hurdles, a fresh start sweeps clean energy into your world, which inspires peace, love, and harmony.

DECEMBER WEEK TWO

You reach a significant turning point soon, this shines a light on intimacy and security. It sees you moving forward in tandem with another. Your emotions are guiding your awareness towards developing a more profound bond. This provides you with expanding horizons which are ever growing, it reminds you of the blessings which surround your world. Synergies of the mind and heart abound, sparks are set to light your life ablaze. An opportunity arrives soon to inspire you to head towards change. This is an inspiring time which motivates you to develop your skills in a new area. It leads to activities which expand your horizons and brings you in contact with interesting folks. Broadening your social circle provides you with ample opportunity to form a close bond with someone who fills the role of a nurturer. You can embrace the changes which surround your world.

DECEMBER WEEK THREE

Expanding your horizons is emphasized. This puts the focus on freedom and abundance. Someone makes an offer which is undoubtedly tempting to you. You actively seek opportunity in your world, and the attention you devote to improving your circumstances provides you with a quality opportunity, you can sink your teeth into. This promptly provides you with an abundant direction you can develop. Your focus is on interpersonal matters, and there is a shining moment which inspires you to expand your horizons. Incredible potential breathes new life into your creative zone. This is a page-turning time. New possibilities blossom in your artistic endeavors. Setting positive intentions plants the seeds that grow into a vital area over the coming months. There is a desire for security and working towards goals with an overall strategy provides you with a substantial result. Your organizational skills streamline and refine your workload.

DECEMBER WEEK FOUR

There is an atmosphere of generosity and celebration. It is a time which creates lively discussions, creative inspiration, and meaningful interactions. You may feel especially nostalgic as you think about the past and all the hurdles you have overcome to reach this point. Your best qualities enter into the spotlight soon, and this draws reliable resources into your world. You obtain external support which enables you to enter a phase of growth and self-expression. This brings a boost into your life and fuels your motivation to keep building stable foundations. An opportunity arrives to direct your attention to a new endeavor which holds tantalizing promise. Events are aligning to provide you with a positive direction. You are going to be blessed with a fresh start that carries a great deal of inspiration to you. You can begin to take the first exciting steps on a new personal journey which holds green meaning to you. Pouring your energy into your own life leads you to a chapter of adventure and expansion. You round the corner and head towards clarity about your life direction.

Dear Reader,

I hope you have enjoyed planning your year with the stars utilizing Astrology and Zodiac influences. Twelve zodiac star sign books are released each year which detail a monthly list of astrological events, and a weekly (four weeks to a month) horoscope. You can find me on my Facebook page:

https://www.facebook.com/Siasoz

Feedback is welcomed and appreciated.

Many Blessings,

Sia Sands

Made in the USA
San Bernardino, CA
23 December 2018